First Facts®

Whales and Dolphins Up Close

BELUGA WHALES UP CLOSE

by Jody Sullivan Rake

Consultant:
Deborah Nuzzolo
Education Manager
SeaWorld, San Diego

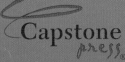

Capstone press®

Mankato, Minnesota

First Facts is published by Capstone Press,
151 Good Counsel Drive, P.O. Box 669, Mankato, Minnesota 56002.
www.capstonepress.com

Library of Congress Cataloging-in-Publication Data
Rake, Jody Sullivan.
    Beluga whales up close / by Jody Sullivan Rake.
    p. cm. — (First facts. Whales and dolphins up close)
    Includes bibliographical references and index.
    Summary: "Presents an up-close look at beluga whales, including their body
features, habitat, and life cycle" — Provided by publisher.
    ISBN-13: 978-1-4296-2263-9 (hardcover)
    ISBN-10: 1-4296-2263-6 (hardcover)
    1. White whale — Juvenile literature. I. Title.
QL737.C433R35 2009
599.5'42 — dc22   2008030102

Editorial Credits
Christine Peterson, editor; Renée T. Doyle, designer; Wanda Winch, photo researcher

Photo Credits
iStockphoto/Klaas Lingbeek-van Kranen, 7 (inset)
marinethemes.com/Kelvin Aitken, 6–7; Kike Calvo, 14 (inset)
Peter Arnold/Fred Bruemmer, 11; Gunter Ziesler, 18
SeaPics.com/Bryan & Cherry Alexander, 21; Doc White, 5; Masa Ushioda, 8 (inset), 14;
    Shedd Aquarium/Brenna Hernandez, 1, 8–9, 17; Ursus/John K. B. Ford, 13
Shutterstock/J. Helgason, 11 (inset); Keo, background throughout; Luis Salazar, 20;
    Timmary, splash element throughout
SuperStock, Inc./Corbis, cover

1 2 3 4 5 6   14 13 12 11 10 09

TABLE OF CONTENTS

Amazing White Whales

Is that an ice chunk floating in the ocean? No, it's a beluga whale. These amazing whales are white from head to tail. Their slippery skin feels squishy, like gelatin.

They may look like ice, but belugas are warm-blooded **mammals**. Like all mammals, belugas breathe air. They give birth to live young.

mammal — a warm-blooded animal that has a backbone

Small Whales

Belugas are smaller than other whales. They are about 13 feet (4 meters) long. That's as long as a pickup truck. Adult belugas weigh about 3,000 pounds (1,360 kilograms). That's as much as its Arctic neighbor the walrus.

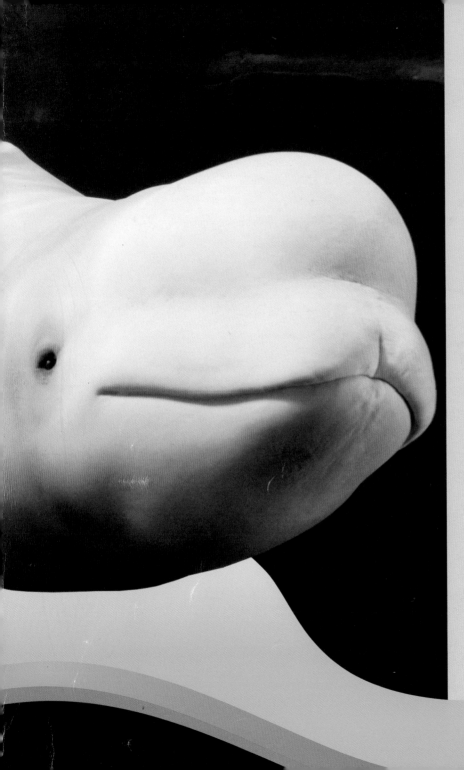

Beached Belugas

Beluga whales often swim near shore in shallow ocean waters. But belugas sometimes swim too close to shore. They can get stuck on land. They have to wait for the tide to come in. When the water rises, belugas swim away.

Neck Bones

Belugas are the only whales that can move their necks. Their neck bones aren't grown together. Belugas sweep their heads back and forth. They nod their heads up and down to find food.

8

Melon Heads

A beluga's head looks small for its body. The blowhole on its head helps it breathe. A beluga's large forehead is called the melon. It is filled with oily fat. The melon makes the beluga's noises sound louder.

Belugas have short snouts that look like big lips. Their mouths have 34 pointed teeth.

Ice Chippers

A **dorsal ridge** runs along a beluga's back. This rough ridge can crack ice. Belugas break thin ice to make breathing holes.

A beluga's tail **flukes** are shaped like a fan. To swim, belugas flip their flukes up and down. Paddle-shaped flippers help them turn.

dorsal ridge — a line of bumps on a beluga's back
fluke — a wide, flat area on a whale's tail

dorsal ridge

fluke

Life in the Arctic

The icy Arctic Ocean is home for beluga whales. They swim near Alaska, Canada, and Russia. Some belugas live in the St. Lawrence River in Canada.

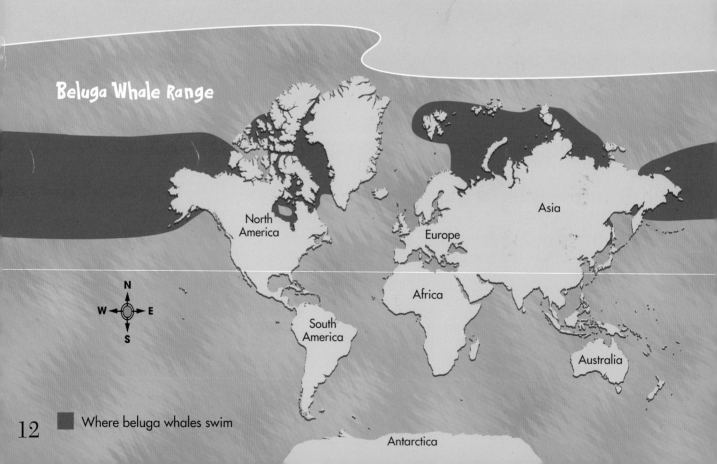

Beluga Whale Range

North America

Europe

Asia

Africa

South America

Australia

Antarctica

N
W E
S

Where beluga whales swim

Blubber keeps belugas warm in icy water. This thick layer of fat makes bulges in their skin. Almost half of a beluga's weight can be blubber.

blubber — a layer of fat under a whale's skin

Big Eaters

Belugas eat a lot of food to build a thick blubber layer. Adult belugas eat about 40 to 50 pounds (18 to 23 kilograms) of food each day. They eat octopus, squid, and fish.

Belugas dive through deep water to find food. They use sharp teeth to snatch **prey**. But belugas don't chew their food. They swallow prey whole.

prey — an animal hunted for food

Beluga Life Cycle

Male and female belugas mate in spring. About 14 months later, a beluga **calf** is born. Beluga calves are about 5 feet (1.5 meters) long. At birth they are dark gray. As they grow, their skin gets lighter and turns white.

Baby belugas have less blubber than adults. They drink rich milk from their mothers to build blubber quickly. Beluga whales live about 30 years.

calf — a baby whale

Life Cycle of a Beluga Whale

Calf

One beluga calf is born at a time.

Young

By age 6, belugas have white skin.

Adult

Adult male and female belugas mate in spring.

Mom and Baby

Pod Talk

Belugas live and swim in groups called **pods**. About 10 belugas live in a pod. In the pod, belugas communicate with clicks, whistles, and other noises. These sounds help pods find food. Clicks and whistles help belugas stay together in their cold ocean home.

pod — a group of whales

Belugas are often called "sea canaries." They make many sounds. Belugas copy noises they hear, even sounds like boat motors. They make noises by moving air around near their blowholes. The oily melon changes shape as the air moves. This movement changes the shape of a beluga's head.

Beluga Whales and People

Arctic natives have hunted belugas for centuries. These people use the oil from a beluga's melon. They make whale skin into leather. Hunters only take a few belugas each year.

Ocean pollution is more harmful to belugas. Many belugas die from pollution. Today laws help protect beluga whales.

Glossary

blubber (BLUH-buhr) — a layer of fat under a whale's skin that protects it from the cold

calf (KAF) — a young whale or dolphin

dorsal ridge (DOR-suhl RIJ) — a line of bumps along a beluga whale's back

fluke (FLOOK) — the wide, flat area at the end of a whale's tail

mammal (MAM-uhl) — a warm-blooded animal that has a backbone

pod (POD) — a group of whales; pods often are made of family members.

prey (PRAY) — an animal hunted by another animal for food

Read More

Herriges, Ann. *Whales*. Oceans Alive. Minneapolis: Bellwether Media, 2007.

Nicklin, Flip, and Linda Nicklin. *Face to Face with Whales*. Face to Face with Animals. Washington, D.C.: National Geographic, 2008.

Squire, Ann O. *Beluga Whales*. A True Book. New York: Children's Press, 2007.

Internet Sites

FactHound offers a safe, fun way to find educator-approved Internet sites related to this book.

Here's what you do:

1. Visit *www.facthound.com*
2. Choose your grade level.
3. Begin your search.

This book's ID number is 9781429622639.

FactHound will fetch the best sites for you!

Index